DEADLY AND INCREDIBLE ANIMALS

TOP 10 Minibeasts

Jay Dale

A+

Smart Apple Media
P.O. Box 3263
Mankato, MN, 56002

First published in 2011 by
MACMILLAN EDUCATION AUSTRALIA PTY LTD
15–19 Claremont St, South Yarra, Australia 3141

Visit our web site at www.macmillan.com.au or go directly to
www.macmillanlibrary.com.au

Associated companies and representatives throughout the world.

Library of Congress Cataloging-in-Publication Data

Dale, Jay.
    Top ten minibeasts / Jay Dale.
        p. cm. — (Deadly and incredible animals)
    Includes index.
    Summary: "Gives general information on features of minibeasts and threats to them. Counts down the top ten most dangerous minibeasts using a deadliness scale"—Provided by publisher.
    ISBN 978-1-59920-411-6 (library binding)
    1. Arachnida—Juvenile literature. 2. Insects—Juvenile literature. 3. Dangerous animals—Juvenile literature. I. Title.
    QL452.2.D35 2012
595—dc22

                              2010049503

Publisher: Carmel Heron
Commissioning Editor: Niki Horin
Managing Editor: Vanessa Lanaway
Proofreader: Georgina Garner
Designer: Cristina Neri, Canary Graphic Design
Page layout: Peter Shaw, Julie Thompson and Cristina Neri
Photo researcher: Legendimages
Illustrator: Andrew Craig and Nives Porcellato
Production Controller: Vanessa Johnson

Manufactured in China by Macmillan Production (Asia) Ltd.
Kwun Tong, Kowloon, Hong Kong
Supplier Code: CP February 2011

Acknowledgments
The author and publisher are grateful to the following for permission to reproduce copyright material:

Front cover photograph: Wolf spider with prey © age fotostock/Emanuele Biggi.

Photographs courtesy of: age fotostock/Emanuele Biggi, **15**; ANTPhoto.com.au/Ken Griffiths, **23**; Australian Red Cross, **30**; Corbis/Esther Beaton, **22**, /ERproductions Ltd/Blend Images, **9**; Dreamstime.com/G3miller, **18**; Aislan Ferreira - Tanooki - Brazil, **24**; Getty Images/Frank Greenaway, **10**, /Time Life Pictures/Carlo Bavagnoli, **4**; Hilary Jones, **11**; naturepl.com/Martin Dohrn, **27**, /PREMAPHOTOS, **26**; NHPA/John Bell, **21**; Photolibrary/Alamy/Buddy Mays, **19**, /Scott Camazine, **17**, /Gregory MD., **3**, **20**, back cover, /John Mitchell, **13**, /OSF/John Brown, **16**, /OSF/Alastair MacEwen, **6**, **28**, **29**; Shutterstock/cyrrpit, **8**, /Henrik Larsson, **14**, /Audrey Snider-Bell, **12**; Techuser, **25**.

While every care has been taken to trace and acknowledge copyright, the publisher tenders their apologies for any accidental infringement where copyright has proved untraceable. They would be pleased to come to a suitable arrangement with the rightful owner in each case.

The publisher would like to thank the Australian Red Cross for their help reviewing the first aid advice in this manuscript.

CONTENTS

GLOSSARY WORDS
When a word is printed in **bold**, you can look up its meaning in the Glossary on page 31.

DEADLY AND INCREDIBLE ANIMALS

Many animals are deadly to other animals. They are deadly to their prey and sometimes even to their **predators**. Over many thousands of years, these animals have developed incredible behaviors and features to find food, to defend themselves from predators, and to protect their young.

Deadly and Incredible Features and Behaviors

Different types of animals have different deadly features and behaviors. Deadly and incredible features include strong jaws, razor-sharp teeth, and stingers or fangs for injecting **venom** into prey. Deadly and incredible behaviors include stalking, hunting, and distracting prey before attacking and killing it.

Animals such as lions use their incredible size and strength to smash, crush and rip apart their prey. Excellent eyesight helps many **nocturnal** animals hunt their prey under the cover of even the darkest night.

The siafu ant uses its powerful jaws to bite into its grasshopper prey.

DEADLY AND INCREDIBLE MINIBEASTS

Minibeasts are some of the world's smallest animals. Although they are small, these incredible animals can be deadly.

What Are Minibeasts?

Minibeasts are small animals such as spiders, bees, worms, scorpions, and snails. They are **invertebrates**. The minibeasts explored in this book belong to the **arthropod** group. An arthropod has a skeleton on the outside of its body (called an exoskeleton), which it sheds as it grows. Arthropods can be sorted into smaller groups, based on their features.

IN THIS BOOK

In this book you will read about the top 10 deadliest minibeasts on Earth — from number 10 (least deadly) to number 1 (most deadly). There are many different opinions about which minibeasts should top this list. The minibeasts in this book have been selected based on their method of capturing, killing, and eating prey.

MINIBEAST GROUPS

Invertebrates

Arthropods

Insects	Arachnids
All adult insects have six legs, and most have wings and three separate body sections (head, **thorax**, and **abdomen**). Examples: • emerald cockroach wasp • Africanized honey bee • siafu ant • Japanese giant hornet	All adult arachnids have two separate body sections (**cephalothorax** and abdomen) and most have eight walking legs. Examples: • goliath birdeater tarantula • wolf spider • black widow spider • deathstalker scorpion • Sydney funnel-web spider • Brazilian wandering spider

Minibeasts have lived on Earth for millions of years. During this time, they have developed deadly and incredible features and behaviors that help them survive.

Hunting for Food

To survive in the environments in which they live, minibeasts need to kill or **paralyze** and then eat their prey. Most minibeasts use fangs or stingers to inject venom into their victims. Some use their **mandibles** to crush their prey.

Spiders, such as the black widow, use a sticky web to trap prey. The spider then uses its fangs to inject poison into the prey. It then turns its prey into liquid and sucks up the remains through hairs on its mouth.

▶ Japanese giant hornets crush their prey, such as bees, using their powerful mandibles.

Protection from Predators

Minibeasts have developed deadly and incredible features and behaviors to protect themselves from larger predators such as snakes and birds. Some spiders have excellent eyesight and only come out at night, while their predators sleep. Other animals, such as the deathstalker scorpion, use their stinger and **camouflage** to protect themselves.

That's Incredible!

Tarantulas release tiny spiked hairs, which land on their prey and make them itchy. The hairs are especially annoying if they are breathed in by the prey, or land in its eyes.

DEADLY FEATURES AND BEHAVIORS

Feature	Behavior or Use of Feature	Minibeast
Large mandibles, pincers, or claws	Crush, hold, and rip prey apart	Siafu ant Deathstalker scorpion Japanese giant hornet
Fangs	Inject venom to paralyse or kill prey	Goliath birdeater tarantula Wolf spider Black widow spider Brazilian wandering spider Funnel-web spider
Camouflage	Hide and stalk	Spiders Scorpions
Excellent eyesight	Find prey at night	Box jellyfish
Stinger	Inject venom	Scorpions Emerald cockroach Wasp Africanized honey bee
Sticky or tangled webs	Trap prey	Spiders

THREATS TO MINIBEASTS

None of the minibeasts featured in this book are threatened or endangered at this time. However, humans cause the biggest threat to many minibeasts.

Habitat Destruction

As the human population increases, the **habitat** of many minibeasts is destroyed. Land is taken over for farming and trees are cut down for wood products and fuel. For example, as the rain forests in South America are cleared, the habitat of the goliath birdeater tarantula and Africanized honey bee is reduced. Flowering trees and shrubs are chopped down, removing their pollen food source. Heavy machinery destroys the tarantulas' burrows.

◄ The birdeater tarantula's natural habitat is being destroyed to make way for farming.

Respecting the Minibeasts' Environments

Bushwalkers, campers, and gardeners need to take great care when visiting, walking, or camping in minibeasts' natural environments.

Here are some basic rules to follow:

1. Watch where you put your feet! Use existing tracks and try to avoid walking through uncleared bushland to reduce the damage to any animal's natural habitat.

2. Do not disturb any wildlife. Remember you are a visitor in their home.

3. If you push over a rock or move some undergrowth, place it back where it was — it may be an animal's home.

4. Take time to admire the wildlife around you from a safe distance.

5. Always take your trash away with you.

Minibeasts can be amazing to look at, but remember to stay a safe distance away — both for their benefit and yours!

FEMALE EMERALD COCKROACH WASP

The female emerald cockroach wasp preys on cockroaches. She uses her venom to sting her prey so the prey can't move. The wasp then lays her egg inside the live cockroach.

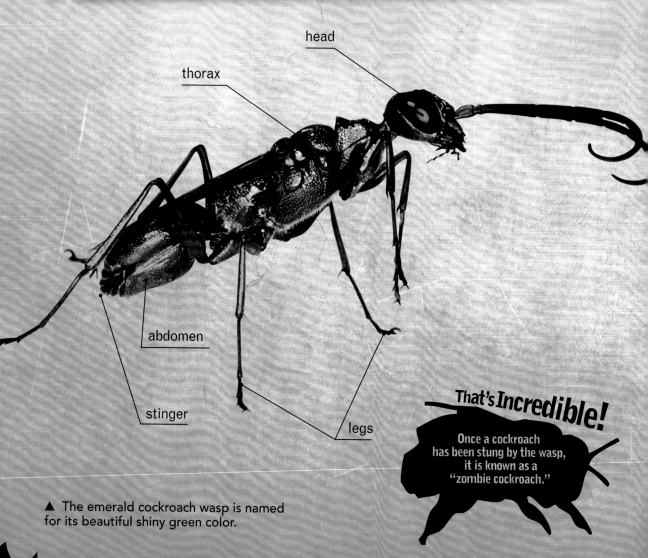

head

thorax

abdomen

stinger

legs

That's Incredible!

Once a cockroach has been stung by the wasp, it is known as a "zombie cockroach."

▲ The emerald cockroach wasp is named for its beautiful shiny green color.

Deadly features: stinger
Predators: unknown
Size: 0.9 inch (22 mm) long
Lifespan: several months
Habitat: underground burrows at the base of trees

Distribution: ◼
tropical regions such as Southeast Asia, Africa, and the Pacific Islands

Controlling its Prey

The emerald cockroach wasp is one of nature's most incredible insects. The female does not kill the prey when it injects it with venom. Instead, the wasp turns the prey into a live food source for its growing young.

What's for Dinner?
Emerald cockroach wasps eat cockroaches.

The emerald cockroach wasp's venom confuses the cockroach so that it does not flee.

Step 1 — day 1
The female emerald cockroach wasp injects venom into the cockroach's thorax and brain, so the cockroach cannot escape.

Step 2 — day 1
The wasp chews off half of each of the cockroach's antennae and then leads it to her burrow, like a dog on a leash.

Step 3 — day 1
In the burrow, the wasp lays an egg on the cockroach's abdomen. She leaves the burrow and blocks the entrance. The cockroach cannot move and stays in the burrow.

Step 4 — days 4–16
The egg hatches. The **larva** feeds on the cockroach for up to 12 days. It eats the cockroach's organs in a special order so the cockroach stays alive.

Step 5 — day 17
The larva spins a cocoon inside the cockroach.

Step 6
Finally, an adult wasp breaks out of the cocoon. It eats the last of the cockroach and crawls out of the burrow.

11

GOLIATH BIRDEATER TARANTULA

The goliath birdeater tarantula is the largest spider in the world. It was given its name when early European explorers to South America saw it feeding on a whole hummingbird.

That's **Incredible!**

Unlike most spiders, the goliath birdeater tarantula can make a noise. When disturbed, it makes a strange hissing sound as it rubs the hairs on its legs together.

eight legs

cephalothorax

spinnerets (to spin silk for webs)

abdomen

chelicerae (jaws), with hollow fangs attached

▲ The goliath birdeater tarantula's venom is harmless to humans, but its large size scares most people.

Deadly features: poisonous barbed hairs, hollow fangs, venom

Predators: humans, tarantula hawk wasps, other tarantula spiders

Size: legs up to 10 inches (25 cm) long; weight up to 6 ounces (170 g); fangs 0.8 to 1.6 in (2–4 cm) long

Lifespan: females 15 to 25 years, males 3 to 6 years

Habitat: deep burrows in swampy areas

Distribution: ■
rain forests of northern South America

Juicy Prey

The goliath birdeater tarantula sneaks up on its prey and kills it with a **venomous** bite. It feels the prey approaching its burrow through vibrations in the ground. It does not have teeth for chewing, so it covers its prey in **digestive juices** to turn it into a liquid. It then sucks up the liquid. When it is finished, only bones, fur, or feathers remain.

Defensive Bite

The goliath birdeater tarantula will only bite a human if it feels threatened. Its bite is similar to a normal wasp bite, causing swelling and mild pain.

What's for Dinner?
Goliath birdeater tarantulas eat insects, other small invertebrates, mice, rats, frogs, small snakes, lizards, bats, and small birds from nests.

▼ The goliath birdeater tarantula uses its fangs to carry prey to a safe place to suck out its insides.

13

WOLF SPIDER

The wolf spider is well known for its speed in chasing its prey over short distances. It is also incredibly acrobatic, often flipping over onto its back to catch prey with its legs.

abdomen

cephalothorax

eight eyes

fangs

eight legs

There are many different **species** of wolf spider found throughout the world.

That's Incredible!

Wolf spiders carry up to 100 eggs in an egg sac. Once they hatch, the spiderlings climb onto their mother's abdomen until they are old enough to hunt for themselves.

Deadly features: fangs, excellent eyesight, fast runner, camouflage

Predators: coyotes, owls, insect predators such as wasps

Size: 0.8 to 1.4 inches (20–35 mm) long

Lifespan: females three to four years, males up to one year

Habitat: shrubland, woodland, coastal forests, under rocks, sometimes underground burrows

Distribution: ■ throughout the world

Night Prowler

Most wolf spiders like to stay hidden during the day. They come out at night to wander the ground, looking for prey. The wolf spider has fantastic eyesight for locating prey in the dark. It uses its fangs to inject venom into its prey. It uses its strong mandibles to crush its prey.

What's for Dinner?

Wolf spiders eat crickets, other spiders, ants, grasshoppers, and small invertebrates. Larger wolf spider species may eat small lizards and frogs.

Lone Wolf

The wolf spider hunts alone. Some wolf spiders hide near the opening of their burrows, ready to pounce on their prey. Wolf spiders that do not make a burrow will hunt and chase their prey.

▼ The wolf spider's venom kills or paralyzes its prey.

AFRICANIZED HONEY BEE

The Africanized honey bee is the world's most **aggressive** bee. It attacks in a large group, and is often called the "killer bee."

▼ It is quite difficult to tell the Africanized honey bee from other honey bee species. Both have six legs, four clear wings, one stinger and a brown and black striped body.

eyes

thorax

head

wings

legs

abdomen

That's Incredible!

African honey bees were brought to South America in 1956. Scientists were trying to breed a honey bee that would suit the South American climate. Some bees escaped and mated with the Brazilian honey bee, resulting in the very aggressive Africanized honey bee.

stinger

Deadly features: aggressive behavior, group attack, stinger

Predators: other aggressive insects, humans

Size: 0.5 inch (13 mm) long

Lifespan: 28 to 35 days (females die after injecting their sting)

Habitat: nests in hollow trees, walls, porches, sheds, attics, garbage bins, and old vehicles

Distribution: ■
South America and southern North America

Do Not Disturb

The Africanized honey bee is deadly to any animal or human that disturbs its hive. Once disturbed, even by the noise from a car, the **colony** will attack in a **swarm**. When one bee stings its prey, it releases chemicals called pheromones (say *feh-reh-mohnz*), which tell the other bees to also sting.

Deadly Defense

Unlike many of the top 10 deadliest minibeasts, the Africanized honey bee is not a meat-eater. It is deadly only when it attacks to protect itself, its colony, and its hive.

What's for Dinner?
Africanized honey bees eat the honey that they make from the nectar of flowers.

▶ A swarm of Africanized honey bees will work together to aggressively defend their hive from attack.

17

6

FEMALE BLACK WIDOW SPIDER

The black widow spider is the third deadliest spider in the world. It gets its name from its strange and deadly mating behavior. Once a female black widow spider has mated, she injects venom into her mate and eats him.

abdomen

spinnerets (to spin silk for webs)

eight legs

chelicerae (jaws) with hollow fangs attached

cephalothorax

That's Incredible!

Baby black widows, called spiderlings, are cannibals and often eat each other!

▲ The red markings on the black widow spider's abdomen are a warning sign of its dangerous venom.

Deadly features: poisonous venom, eats male after mating, tangled web

Predators: praying mantis, birds

Size: 1.5 inches (38 mm) long; abdomen about 0.3 inch (6.4 mm) round

Lifespan: one to three years

Habitat: dark, damp places such as in drainpipes, and under logs and rocks

Distribution: ■
many **temperate** regions around the world

Tangled Web

The female black widow spider spins a large, tangled web close to the ground, to snare insects. Sometimes she attaches one sticky thread to the ground. When this thread is triggered by an insect, it flicks up and flings up the insect for the spider to catch midair.

No Escape

Once an insect is caught in a black widow spider's web, there is no escape. Using little hairs on her hind legs, she covers her prey in silk, so it cannot move. She then bites the insect with her fangs and injects venom and digestive juices into its body. This turns the insect's flesh into a liquid, so she can suck it up to feed.

What's for Dinner?

Female black widow spiders eat male black widow spiders and insects such as mosquitoes, flies, or beetles.

▼ The female black widow spider traps prey in the sticky silk of her tangled web.

DEATHSTALKER SCORPION

The deathstalker scorpion kills its prey with the venom in its tail stinger. Its venom is deadly, but it might also be useful. Scientists believe the venom could be used to treat brain tumors.

That's Incredible!

Scorpions lived on Earth more than 430 million years ago—well before the dinosaurs.

telson (tail)

extended abdomen, covered by an exoskeleton

cephalothorax

several pairs of smaller eyes

two large eyes

pectines (feelers that smell prey)

▲ The scorpion has feelers called pectines on its abdomen, which are used to "smell" prey.

legs

pincers

Deadly features: deadly tail stinger, camouflage
Predators: meerkats, mongooses, owls, lizards, spiders, and other scorpions
Size: 3.5 to 4.5 inches (9–11.5 cm) long
Lifespan: two to six years
Habitat: under stones and rocks in sandy deserts and scrublands

Distribution: ■
Northern Africa and the Middle East

Deadliest Stinger

Although smaller than most scorpions, the deathstalker scorpion has the deadliest venom of all scorpions. This is unusual, because it has quite a thin tail. Normally, scorpions that have a fat tail have the strongest venom, but the deathstalker breaks this rule!

Sneaky Predator

The deathstalker scorpion blends in very well to its sandy, desert habitat, so it can sneak up on its prey. The scorpion grabs prey with its pincers, then quickly strikes with its tail stinger. It then sprays the victim with an acid to turn it into liquid, and eats it.

What's for Dinner?
Deathstalker scorpions eat smaller scorpions, spiders, and insects.

▶ The deathstalker scorpion's deadly stinger is on the end of its curved tail.

21

MALE SYDNEY FUNNEL-WEB SPIDER

The male Sydney funnel-web is the deadliest of the 40 different species of the Australian funnel-web spider. Some scientists believe it is the second deadliest spider on Earth, because it is deadly to humans, apes, monkeys, and insects.

▼ The male Sydney funnel-web spider has six joints on each of its eight legs. That makes 48 knees altogether!

eight legs

chelicerae (jaws) with hollow fangs attached

large venomous fangs

spur (used to hold the female during mating)

That's Incredible!

Rabbits, mice, cats, and dogs are not affected by the funnel-web spider's venom. They can often survive 100 times more venom than it takes to kill a human.

cephalothorax

abdomen

spinnerets (to spin silk for webs)

Deadly features: powerful fangs up to 0.3 inch (7 mm) long for injecting venom

Predators: birds and lizards

Size: between 0.4 and 1 inch (1–2.5 cm) long

Lifespan: up to eight years

Habitat: small, round burrows lined with silk in moist, cool, and sheltered places, such as under rocks or rotting logs

Distribution: ■
Sydney, Australia

Tripping Prey

The male funnel-web spider ambushes its prey using silk trip lines outside its burrow. It hides just inside the burrow with its legs on the trip lines. When it senses prey approaching, it races out and catches the prey. Then, it drags the stunned animal into its burrow to eat it.

A Venomous Bite

The funnel-web spider has a strong, forceful bite. It raises the front of its body and strikes downward. Before it bites, venom forms in beads on its fangs. As the fangs sink into the prey, the venom is forced into the wound.

What's for Dinner?

Sydney funnel-web spiders eat insects and their **larvae**, snails, small frogs, lizards, and millipedes.

▼ The spider raises itself up before it bites. The bite of the male Sydney funnel-web spider is far more venomous than a bite from the female.

23

BRAZILIAN WANDERING SPIDER

The Brazilian wandering spider is an aggressive and fast-moving hunter. It has caused more human deaths than any other spider on Earth.

▼ The Brazilian wandering spider displays its red mouth parts when it is angry.

That's Incredible!

The Brazilian wandering spider is also known as the banana spider because it hides in banana plants. Some spiders have even traveled to other parts of the world hidden in boxes of bananas!

abdomen

cephalothorax

eight legs

eight eyes

chelicerae (jaws) with hollow fangs attached

Deadly features: deadly venom

Predators: birds, lizards

Size: leg length 5 to 6 inches (13–15 cm); body length 0.6 to 2 inches (15–50 mm)

Lifespan: one to two years

Habitat: banana plants, termite mounds, or under rotting logs or rocks in warm, moist jungle areas

Distribution: ■
jungles of South America

On the Prowl

The Brazilian wandering spider prowls the dark, moist jungle floor looking for prey. When it finds its prey, it injects the prey with a venom that turns it into a liquid. The spider then sucks up the prey with little effort.

▼ When it is about to attack, the Brazilian wandering spider rears up on its hind legs and sways from side to side.

The Attack Pose

If it is disturbed, the Brazilian wandering spider raises up its front legs, ready to attack. From this defense position it shows its red mouth parts. The Brazilian wandering spider hides during the day in dark places, such as in piles of leaves.

What's for Dinner?
Brazilian wandering spiders eat crickets, other large insects, small lizards, and small mice.

SIAFU ANT

The siafu ants of Africa attack their prey in one large moving swarm. They can climb quietly onto a person without them knowing. One leader ant sends out a signal and every ant bites at the same time, causing incredible pain. Once the ants' jaws are locked into flesh, they will not let go!

head

legs

thorax

mandibles

abdomen

That's Incredible!

African villagers quickly leave when a large siafu ant swarm arrives in their village. The ants attack all the pests in the village, and the villagers move back into pest-free houses.

▲ Siafu ants use their large and powerful mandibles to bite, crush, and tear their prey to pieces.

Deadly features: large mandibles, swarming to kill other animals

Predators: unknown

Size: worker ants up to 0.2 inch (5 mm) long; soldier ants up to 0.6 inch (15 mm) long; queen ant up to 2 inches (50 mm) long

Lifespan: 3 to 13 months

Colony size: up to 22 million ants; the queen lays up to 2 million eggs every month

Habitat: nests underground or in the holes of trees

Distribution: ■
Western
Africa
and the
Congo

Group hunters

Siafu ants hunt in swarms about 1 foot (30 cm) wide and up to 230 feet (70 m) long. They eat any living thing in their way – usually insects and spiders, and sometimes small mammals. The ants rip their prey apart and pass the pieces to the queen at the back of the swarm.

Teamwork

The worker ants at the front of the swarm kill most of the prey. The ants behind them are soldier ants, which guard the worker ants and the prey. The soldier ants catch any prey that escapes from the worker ants.

What's for dinner?

Siafu ants eat insects, spiders, scorpions, small mammals, lizards and snakes.

▲ When the worker siafu ants have killed the prey, the rest of the ants swarm to feed.

JAPANESE GIANT HORNET

The Japanese giant hornet is the world's largest and deadliest wasp. One of these wasps can attack and kill up to 40 honey bees per minute. It does not always sting its victims — most often it rips the heads and limbs off its prey.

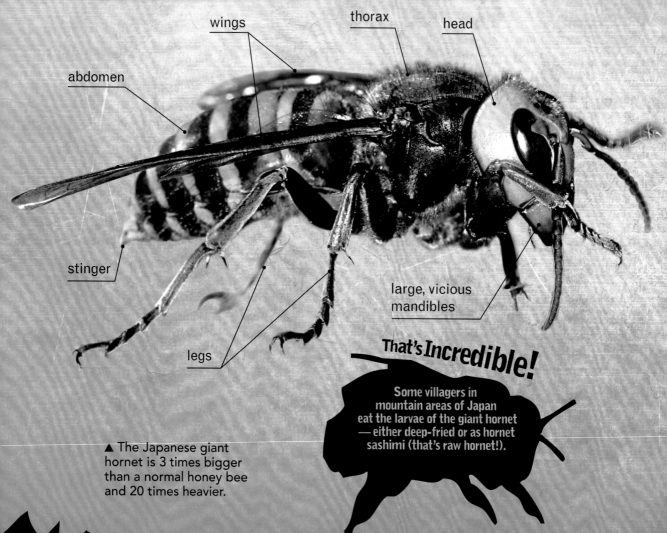

wings

thorax

head

abdomen

stinger

large, vicious mandibles

legs

▲ The Japanese giant hornet is 3 times bigger than a normal honey bee and 20 times heavier.

That's Incredible!

Some villagers in mountain areas of Japan eat the larvae of the giant hornet —either deep-fried or as hornet sashimi (that's raw hornet!).

Deadly features: large stinger that is 0.2 inch (6 mm) long for injecting venom, giant mandibles, ability to travel quickly over long distances

Predators: praying mantis (which does not always win the fight)

Size: queen 2 inches (5.5 cm) long; worker 1 to 1.8 inches (25–45 mm) long; wingspan up to 3 inches (7.5 cm)

Lifespan: 6 to 12 months

Habitat: nests in trees in forested and mountainous areas of Japan

Distribution: ■
Japan

On the Hunt

The Japanese giant hornet prefers to prey on honey bees and smaller wasps. The hornet sends out scouts to find a bee colony. Once found, the hornet scouts give off a chemical which attracts other hornets to the nest.

Violent Attack

The Japanese giant hornet uses its mandibles to crush the bees and rip them apart. Once all the bees in the hive have been killed, the hornets feed on the honey and take the bee larvae back for the young hornets to eat.

▶ The Japanese giant hornet uses its strong mandibles and sharp black tooth to crush and rip apart its prey.

What's for Dinner?
Japanese giant hornets eat honey bees, smaller hornets, wasps, praying mantises, and beetles.

FIRST AID

Keep these first aid tips in mind if you are bitten by a minibeast. Quick action can help minimize the impact of stings and bites.

First aid when bitten by a funnel-web spider

1 Keep the person calm, reassured, and still.
2 Apply firm pressure over the bite area. Use your hand if necessary.
3 Using firm pressure, apply a bandage over the bite or sting area.
4 For a bite on the arm or leg, apply another bandage. Starting near the fingers or toes, firmly bandage upward, covering as much of the limb as possible. Keep the limb still by using a splint.
5 Seek medical help immediately.
6 Monitor the person and give CPR if needed.

First aid when stung by a scorpion

1 Apply a wrapped ice-pack over the bite site.
2 Raise the injured area.
3 Seek medical advice.

First aid when stung by a wasp, bee, or ant

1 If the person is **allergic** to an ant, bee, or wasp sting, seek medical help immediately. The person may carry medication that they can take.
2 If the sting remains in the skin, remove by scraping it away. Do not squeeze it.
3 If the person is not allergic to an ant, bee, or wasp sting, apply an ice-pack to reduce pain. Seek medical help if the pain continues.

GLOSSARY

Abdomen The back part of an arthropod's body

Aggressive Angry and often ready to attack

Allergic Having a strong reaction to something such as an insect bite, causing the face and airways to swell, making breathing difficult

Arthropod An invertebrate that has jointed limbs, a segmented body, and an external skeleton

Camouflage Spots, stripes, other patterns or colors on an animal that allow it to blend in with its environment

Cephalothorax The combined head and thorax of an arachnid

Colony Group of insects, such as bees or ants, that live close together

Digestive juices Juices from the stomach and mouth, such as saliva

Endangered In danger of becoming extinct (wiped out)

Habitat The environment where animals and plants live

Invertebrates Animals without a backbone, such as insects and spiders

Larva (plural: larvae) Insect young

Mandibles Pincers near an arthropod's mouth, used to cut, grasp, or crush food

Nocturnal Active (usually hunting) at night

Paralyse Make the body unable to move

Predators Meat-eating animals that hunt, kill, and eat other animals

Species A group of animals or other living things that share similar features and behaviors

Swarm Large group of insects

Temperate From the mild climate regions, between the tropical and polar regions

Thorax The middle part of an insect's body behind the head, where the legs attach

Tropical From the warm climate region around the middle of Earth, near the Equator

Venom A poisonous or harmful substance produced by an animal, which is injected by a bite or a sting

Venomous Contains harmful poison, called venom

INDEX